Lisa Trumbauer

A monkey uses its tail
to swing.

A possum uses its tail
to cling.

A kangaroo uses its tail to hop.

A horse uses its tail
to swat.

A whale uses its tail
to slap.

A fox uses its tail
to nap.

My dog uses his tail
to say hello.
And this is the best tail
that I know.